MARGARET MORGAN
and
MARY MORGAN PEDLOW

Memorial

RIVERSIDE   PUBLIC   LIBRARY

THE ANCIENT WORLD

The Mayas

THE ANCIENT WORLD

The Mayas

Pamela Odijk

Silver Burdett Press

Acknowledgments

The author and publishers are grateful to the following for permission to reproduce copyright photographs and prints:

ANT/NHPA pp. 12; Michael Holford pp. 11, 13, 14, 19, 20, 27, 28, 29, 31, 32, 39 and the cover photograph; South American Pictures pp. 10, 22, 38; Werner Forman Archive pp. 15, 16, 18, 21, 23, 24, 25, 26, 33, 35, 36, 37; World Vision p. 41.

While every care has been taken to trace and acknowledge copyright, the publishers tender their apologies for any accidental infringement where copyright has proven untraceable. They would be pleased to come to a suitable arrangement with the rightful owner in each case.

First published 1989 by
THE MACMILLAN COMPANY OF AUSTRALIA PTY LTD
107 Moray Street, South Melbourne 3205
6 Clarke Street, Crows Nest 2065

Adapted and first published in the United States in 1990
by Silver Burdett Press, Englewood Cliffs, N.J.

Library of Congress Cataloging-in-Publication Data

Odijk, Pamela, 1942–
    The Mayas / by Pamela Odijk.
        p.   cm.—(The Ancient world)
    "First published 1989 by the Macmillan Company of
Australia... adapted and first published in the United States in
1990"—T.p. verso.
    Summary: Describes the Mayan civilization which flourished in
southern Mexico and Central America from 250 to 850.
    1. Mayas—Juvenile literature. [1. Mayas. 2. Indians of
Central America.] I. Title. II. Series: Odijk, Pamela,
1942–   Ancient world.
    F1435.O28   1990
    972.81′.016—dc20   89-39567
    ISBN 0-382-09890-0   CIP
                                              AC

Printed in Hong Kong

The Mayas

Contents

The Mayas: Timeline

It is believed that the ancestors of the Mayas came from Asia thousands of years ago when Asia and North America were joined by a land bridge.

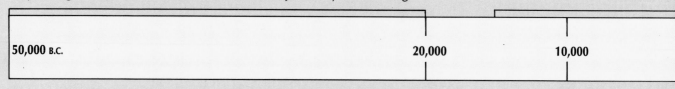

50,000 B.C.   20,000   10,000

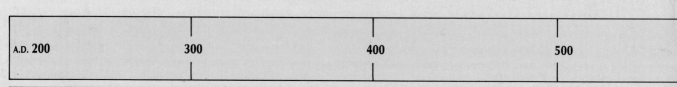

A.D. 200   300   400   500

Classic period: many farming communities had been established on the Yucatan Peninsula. Many of the great Maya cities were built, including Tikal, which covered an area of 6 square miles (16 square kilometers).

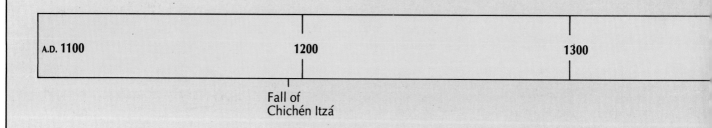

A.D. 1100   1200   1300

Fall of
Chichén Itzá

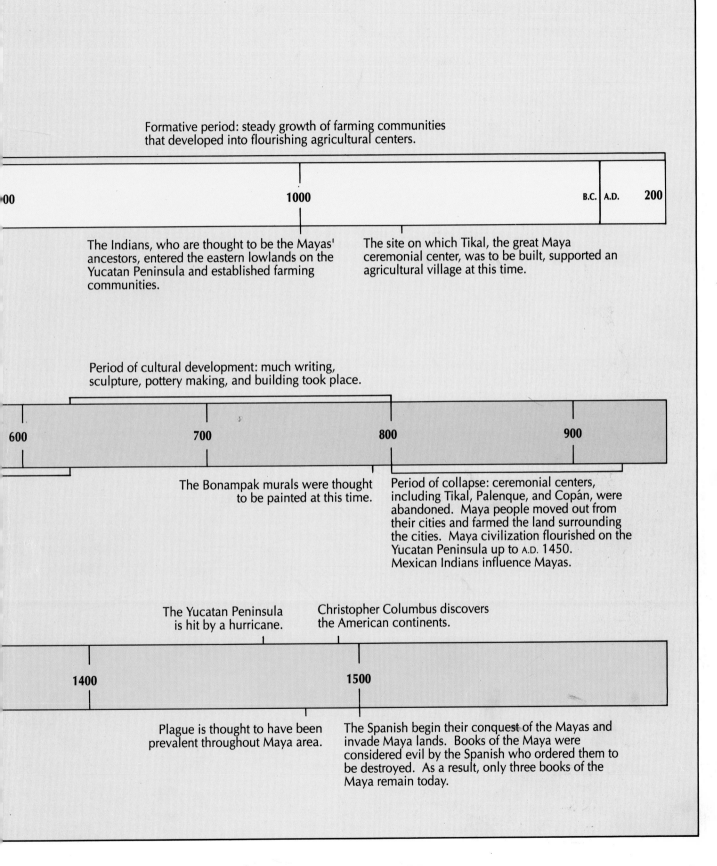

Formative period: steady growth of farming communities that developed into flourishing agricultural centers.

00   1000   B.C. A.D. 200

The Indians, who are thought to be the Mayas' ancestors, entered the eastern lowlands on the Yucatan Peninsula and established farming communities.

The site on which Tikal, the great Maya ceremonial center, was to be built, supported an agricultural village at this time.

Period of cultural development: much writing, sculpture, pottery making, and building took place.

600   700   800   900

The Bonampak murals were thought to be painted at this time.

Period of collapse: ceremonial centers, including Tikal, Palenque, and Copán, were abandoned. Maya people moved out from their cities and farmed the land surrounding the cities. Maya civilization flourished on the Yucatan Peninsula up to A.D. 1450. Mexican Indians influence Mayas.

The Yucatan Peninsula is hit by a hurricane.

Christopher Columbus discovers the American continents.

1400   1500

Plague is thought to have been prevalent throughout Maya area.

The Spanish begin their conquest of the Mayas and invade Maya lands. Books of the Maya were considered evil by the Spanish who ordered them to be destroyed. As a result, only three books of the Maya remain today.

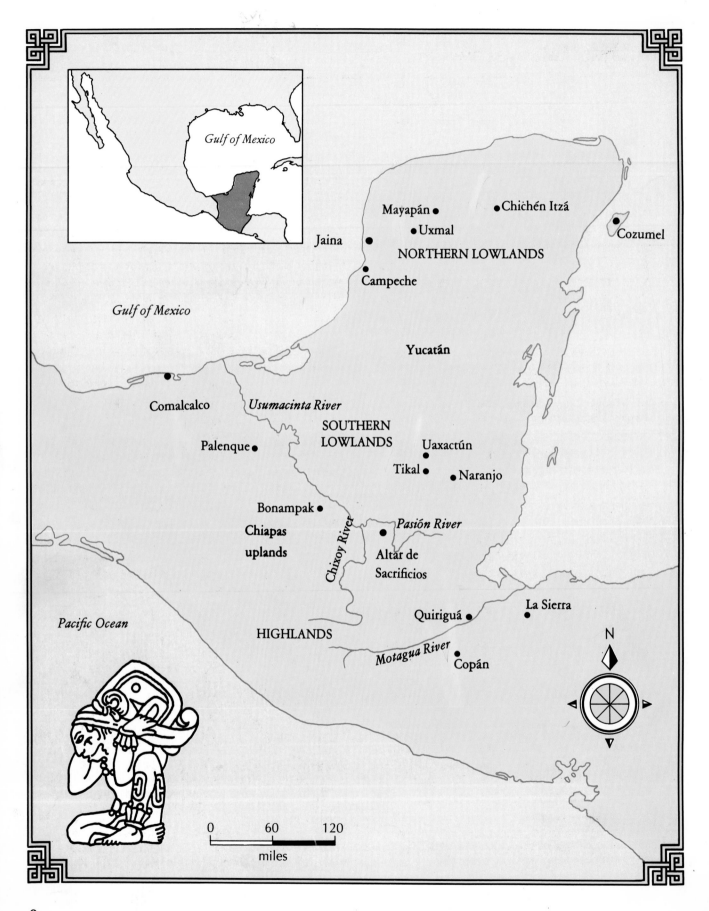

Gulf of Mexico

Gulf of Mexico

Jaina ●

Mayapán ●   ● Chichén Itzá

● Uxmal

Cozumel

NORTHERN LOWLANDS

● Campeche

Yucatán

Comalcalco ●

Usumacinta River

SOUTHERN
LOWLANDS

Palenque ●

Uaxactún ●
Tikal ●   ● Naranjo

Bonampak ●

Chixoy River

Pasión River

Chiapas
uplands

● Altar de
Sacrificios

Pacific Ocean

Quiriguá ●   ● La Sierra

HIGHLANDS

Motagua River   ● Copán

N

0   60   120

miles

The Mayas: Introduction

The ancient Mayas lived in present-day southern Mexico, Belize, Guatemala, Honduras, and western El Salvador. When the Spanish arrived in Central America and Mexico in the sixteenth century, the Mayas occupied lands shown on the map opposite.

The Mayas were so culturally advanced that they have been compared to the Greeks of the Old World. They were fine farmers and architects. They built magnificent pyramids and temples. They were also fine artists, goldsmiths, and coppersmiths. Their social system, based on their beliefs and ideas, ensured harmony with the environment.

Maya writing is a kind of hieroglyphic writing. Today, many of the hieroglyphs can be read. The ancient Maya texts tell us about many aspects of Maya culture and history—even the names of ancient rulers.

For the Mayas, time was of great importance. Many of their **stelae**, altars, and books marked the passage of time. The Mayas believed in the eternity of time, respected it, measured it, and recorded it. The Mayas developed their own calendar, probably based on ones used by earlier peoples who had lived nearby.

Some great Maya cities developed during the Formative period, but it was during the Classic period that the Maya civilization reached its peak and the greatest cities flourished. During that time, Maya lands were divided into powerful city-states, each ruled by a city. One of the largest of these centers was Tikal, in Guatemala's northern Petén. The excavated center has thousands of structures, from tiny house mounds to gigantic temples and palaces. Some important Classic Maya sites are Palenque and Coba in Mexico and Copán in Honduras. The stone walls at some sites are decorated with murals and carvings that show human **sacrifice** and other details of Maya life.

Jade was the Mayas' most precious stone, quantities of which have been found buried with the Maya elite in tombs.

Some of the neighbors of the Maya in Mexico and Central America also developed advanced cultures. The Mayas had constant contact with these groups, traded with them, and exchanged knowledge. Beginning in about A.D. 790, and extending to A.D. 900, the great Maya lowland civilization went into a decline and change from which it never recovered. Explanations for this are still being sought.

Today, descendants of the Maya people still live in parts of Central America and Mexico. Many tend their crops and dress in very much the same way as their ancestors. They practice old religions before their altars, even though Christianity is the accepted religion. Although no modern civilization is a living relic of its ancestors, we see a resemblance to the past in the modern Mayas.

The Mayas were not completely conquered by the Spanish until 1697. With this, their civilization and spirit were not broken, but evolved into the Maya culture of today.

History of the Mayas

The history of the Mayas is usually broken down into the following periods:

Formative Period   c 2000 B.C.–c A.D. 250
Includes the rise of powerful rulers and the development of cities.

Classic   c A.D. 250–900
The greatest era of sculpture, writing, building, and pottery.

Postclassic   c A.D. 900–1540
Many Classic-period centers abandoned. Spanish influence begins in sixteenth century.

The Importance of Landforms and Climate

The landforms and climate of any area determine, to a large extent, how the people live, what kinds of crops can be grown, and what kinds of animals are native to the area.

The southern Maya area, the highlands of Chiapas and Guatemala, is mountainous with high volcanic peaks. In between these peaks are valleys and sprawling plateaus. The soil is rich and fertile. The north has well-drained slopes. The Chiapas Uplands rise gradually to 5,000 feet (1,500 meters).

The Mayas made use of the area's volcanic rock. **Obsidian** was used to make knives and spears. **Volcanic tuff** was sometimes used for building. **Iron pyrite** was used for mirrors, and deposits of **specular hematite** were used to make red paint. Some small deposits of gold, copper, and jade also existed.

The central area is a low-lying country of **limestone** from 100–600 feet (30–180 meters) above sea level with many rivers and some lakes. It is covered by forest and savanna. The main rivers are the Usumacinta, the Pasión, and the Chixoy.

Temperatures are mild to hot, as the whole region lies within the tropics. Rainfall in the south is high from June to December, with a dry period from January to May. During the rainy months, rivers flood and swamps become large, flat areas of water. The area of the Yucatan Peninsula in the north is drier: rain soaks through the limestone bedrock, leaving little surface water, but the water table feeds natural wells called **cenotes.**

Salt deposits are found in the coastal regions of Yucatan, along the Pacific Coast and the northern fringes of the highlands.

Opposite: Temple of the Sun at Palenque. Much of the land once inhabited by the Mayas is covered in dense rain forest.

Below: in between the high mountains of Guatemala are valleys with sprawling plateaus through which many rivers run.

Natural Plants, Animals, and Birds

Most of the lands once inhabited by the Mayas are covered with rain forest. Around Tikal the vast tropical rain forest has trees up to 150 feet (45 meters) high. Here grow mahogany, cedar, **ceiba,** many varieties of palms (some of which were used for thatched roofs), and the sapodilla (from which a sap to make gum was obtained). The food-producing breadnut tree, vanilla vines, and rubber trees, plus many climbing and flowering plants, including orchids, are also found here. Vines were used for house frames, baskets, wickerwork, rope, and twine. Some provided a source of water for travelers or workers in the forest.

To enable crops to be grown, the Mayas had to clear this forest with primitive tools. Axes and fire were the main tools. The land would be cultivated for one or two years, after which the soil's nutrients were depleted. A new area would need to be cleared, a practice called slash-and-burn farming.

During Maya times, forest animals included deer, **peccary**, wild pigs, **agouti, sloth,** rabbits, foxes, monkeys, and jaguars. There were also boas, rattlesnakes, coral snakes, and many species of lizards, toads, and frogs. Bird life was plentiful and included parrots, wild turkeys, **curassows,** toucans, and red-breasted **trogons**.

In the Chiapas Uplands, there were pine and savanna-covered plateaus and belts of live oak. The central area of Petén had infertile soil and few usable plants. In the Maya highlands lived the quetzal bird, whose long blue-green tail feathers were highly prized.

The three-toed sloth inhabits the forests where the Mayas once lived.

Crops and Hunting

Crops

Maya farmers probably worked the soil and sowed the crops under the direction of the elite. The Mayas, like other agricultural people, had a great love of the soil. Maize, which was their main food crop, was sacred. Farmers worked according to their religious beliefs. Every stage of farming was interwoven with religious celebration. Before the land was cleared, the Mayas made offerings of prayers, candles, flowers, and food to the gods. All cultivation in the fields was done by people using hand tools. There were no beasts of burden or plows. Boys were expected to work in the fields. Girls helped the women in the house.

After crops were planted, prayers would be offered to the red rain god. From time to time human sacrifices would be offered to the rain god as well. Besides maize, cultivated beans, squashes, **chilies, maguey, manioc,** and **cacao** were grown. Because of the growth of weeds and the declining fertility of the soil, farmers frequently had to seek and clear new areas farther away from their settlements.

Swamps

In areas where there were swamps, the Mayas often made good use of the land. In some places, soil and other matter were piled on parts of the swamp to make fertile beds where crops could be grown. The Mayas planted cotton and fruit trees as well as other crops. Canals in between drained the swampland and provided water for irrigation. **Balche,** a sacred drink, was made from one kind of tree.

Sculpture perhaps representing a messenger who delivered prayers to the rain gods.

Hunting

Hunters went out with bows and arrows, traps, spears, and netting bags to hunt deer and other game. The proper rituals had to be performed for a successful hunt. These probably included prayers and offerings of food. Dogs trained to help in the hunt probably accompanied their masters. When a deer was killed, the hunter would kneel beside it and apologize for his action. He offered the animal's spirit as an explanation for the killing—he needed the meat for food.

When the hunter returned, the meat was shared with other families and the hides cured. Wild pigs, rabbits, squirrels, and turkeys and other birds were also hunted. Clay pellets shot from blow guns may have been used to kill small birds.

Along the coast, fish, shellfish, and turtles were caught and collected. In some places bees were kept for honey and wax.

How Families Lived

Houses

Houses varied from very simple, single-room dwellings of the ordinary people to imposing stone buildings in which the nobility lived. Houses of the nobility and palaces of the rulers had many large rooms. Usually these palaces included rooms used as administrative offices. Ordinary houses had a family **ossuary** beneath the floor.

Maya houses were built with wooden posts supporting a thatched roof. The Mayas who lived in the lowlands often built their houses on low rectangular mounds of earth above the reach of flood waters. During the Formative period, this same type of structure was often built on flat-topped pyramids to serve as temples. An excavated house at La Sierra had two rooms with thick walls built of cobbles set in mortar and a paved floor.

Some houses were built as club houses for unmarried men undergoing informal social and religious education and others for unmarried girls of noble birth.

Houses for families were located near a good water source. Homes were arranged around an open space that was rectangular in design. Clusters of these arrangements formed hamlets in rural areas. For every fifty to one hundred dwellings, there was a minor ceremonial center. Planning of towns did not seem to involve neatly laying out streets.

Families

Upon marriage during late adolescence, a young man was required to live with his wife's family for a period of service that lasted for about six years. After this the couple would live with or near the husband's family. Divorce was recognized in Maya society for several reasons. A Maya woman, for example, could be divorced for not producing children to work with her husband in the fields.

Women and men could own property, and this could be passed on from father to son or from mother to daughter. People took family names for identification and social status. In addition they took a **naal,** or house name, from their mother. This name could only be passed on via the female line.

Left: jade pectoral ornament showing seated Maya noble, from A.D. 600-800.

Opposite: figurine of an important person in full regalia. This sculpture is made from terra-cotta.

Above: cylindrical Maya drinking vessel.

Below: peasant house and furniture.

Mothers brought up their girls strictly, and when they were old enough a marriage was arranged. Marriages could not take place between people with the same family name. Children of the nobility eventually had careers in politics, commerce, or the priesthood. Extreme contrasts in wealth and social status separated the nobility from ordinary Maya families.

Archaeological findings and documents tell us a great deal about education in Maya society. Maya writing shows that the children of the nobility and rulers were taught to read and write.

Furniture

Furniture in peasant homes was simple. It consisted mainly of wooden tables, benches and stools, and beds made of frames resting on slats with a reed mat.

Food and Medicine

Food was cooked and served in pottery utensils. Bowls, colanders, and drinking vessels were made from hollow gourds. People ate simple, frugal meals of stews and vegetables spiced with chilies. Maize was the main food. It was washed and ground into flour with grinding stones, and then made into **tortillas** with water. These were cooked over a fire on a hot griddle and eaten with beans and chili. Maize was also made into **atole, posol,** and **tamale.** Other vegetables, such as squash and wild greens, also were eaten. Game, such as deer, rabbit, and wild turkey, was hunted for food. Honey was eaten and used with the bark of a tree to make a strong sacred drink called balche. Fruits, including papaya (paw paw), aguacate (avocado pear), custard apples, and the fruit of the cacao tree, were also part of the Mayas' diet.

Cacao was not only a food. Cacao beans were used as currency in Mexico and Central America. The beans were made into chocolate drinks only for the elite. Cacao only grows in tropical areas that have high rainfall.

Medicine

The ancient Mayas knew their environment and looked for omens or signs in most things. Sickness and disease were thought to have been "sent" or to have been caused by "evil winds" as a punishment. The **Hmen** were the sorcerers and medicine men, who were both prophets and healers of disease. They made use of potions, chants, prayers, and traditional herbal medicines. Tobacco was an important plant cultivated for ritual and medicinal use. The Mayas were very interested in the medicinal properties of plants, and there is a considerable amount of medical literature from later times that is written in Yucatec with European characters. Most of this literature reports on the effects of certain plants on humans.

Woman grinding maize with stone.

Clothes

Sisal (henequen) and cotton were used to make the simple clothing worn by most people. Carvings and murals show that only nobles wore elaborate clothes, often using particular kinds of clothing for certain ceremonies.

It is thought that tie-dyeing, tapestry, quilting, and a special weaving technique that resembled embroidery were used for making clothes and other textiles.

Early Spanish writers noted that feathers were woven into garments of the nobility, and some Maya sculptures show this. Few Maya textiles have survived, but stelae and **murals** show people wearing fabrics of beautiful designs. No Maya feathered cloaks or headdresses of quetzal plumes have survived.

A section of a mural showing the judgment of captives shows men in short tunics and short, draped cloaks of jaguar skin. Their head-dress is elaborate and is made to look like animals. Other stelae show nobles wearing elaborate maize headdresses and monster headdresses.

Other murals of similar events show spectators in long white robes.

Ornament

Jade was the stone most prized by the Mayas and from it skilled craftspeople fashioned beautiful beads, pendants, and ear ornaments. Some people had their teeth inlaid with pieces of jade. Royal people were buried wearing elaborate jewelry made of jade.

Opposite: relief of jaguar from Chichén Itzá.

Below: women wove the cloth that was used for making clothes.

Religion and Rituals of the Mayas

Every act of Maya life had a religious connection. Prayers and rituals were all a part of everyday life and were carried out with precision, for the Maya believed that all life was in the hands of divine powers. Our knowledge of Maya religion comes mainly from surviving Maya art and writing as well as descriptions the Christian Spanish wrote when they conquered and settled these lands.

Some Maya books, called codices, have calendars and indicate the proper ceremonies and offerings for certain days. These books were probably used by the priests, or Hmen.

It is known that the Mayas had many gods, some of which have been identified.

Maya Gods	
Itzamná	The supreme god of creation, lord of fire and earth. His name means Lizard House.
Ix Chel	Moon goddess, patroness of weaving, **divination**, medicine, and childbirth.
Kukulcán	The feathered serpent, god of the kings; the Maya version of Quetzalcoatl (an Aztec god).

Added to these were gods of the stars, planets, months, days, and maize.

The Chacs were the rain gods.

The Earth and the Universe

Maya art depicts the earth as a giant saurian (lizard or crocodile) floating on a pond with waterlilies and fish. The Mayas thought of the universe as having four world directions, each of which was assigned a different color:

East—red
North—white
West—black
South—yellow

At each of the four sides of the world stood a sacred ceiba tree called "tree of abundance" from which everything came. A fifth green tree was believed to be in the center. The Mayas also believed that there was a heaven of thirteen layers above the earth. Beneath the earth was an underworld composed of nine layers. After death, it was believed that the soul undertook a dangerous journey through the underworld, which was ruled by a number of gods, many of whom were depicted as part man and part jaguar. The jaguar was always associated with the night and the sinister.

Burial and Ancestor Worship

Peasants were buried in very simple graves under the floors of houses. Wealthy people were buried in tombs along with offerings, among them jewelry, pottery, and food. Ancestor worship was common, and a great deal of attention was paid to the royal dead, who were supposed to rejoin the gods.

Below: relief of ruler with prisoner or victim for sacrifice.

Opposite: a ruler of Yaxchilan, Shield Jaguar, holds a flaming torch. His wife, Lady Xoc, kneels before him and pulls a rope barbed with thorns through her tongue. Rulers and their families made painful blood sacrifices as offerings to the Maya gods.

Tomb in the Temple of Inscriptions at Palenque.

Sacrifices

Human sacrifice was a common practice. Captives, and chosen victims were continually offered to the gods. These sacrifices were made because the Mayas believed that the gods needed human blood to become strong and, in turn, serve the people. They believed that sacrifice was for the benefit of all people and the environment. Self-torture was practiced as a form of sacrifice.

The Priesthood

It is probable that only the nobility served as priests. Sons may have succeeded fathers into this office. Maya priesthood was organized along the following lines:

The Maya Priesthood	
Ah Kin Mai or Ahau Kan Mai	Chief priest who was also an administrator. His duties were to examine priests and send them to where they were needed. He also taught writing, **genealogy,** ceremonies for curing illness, computations, astronomy, astrology, divination, and religious ritual.
Ah Kin	Regular priests who made divinations and sacrifices. The treatment of sickness was an important priestly duty.
Chilans	Prophets and soothsayers. It is thought that the visions of the chilans were induced by drugs and hallucinogenic mushrooms.
Nacons	Special priests whose duty was to remove the hearts of sacrificial victims.

Obeying the Law

The Maya rulers and religion controlled people's lives. Along with their priestly roles, rulers were thought to have godlike qualities, which supposedly came from their divine ancestry. The ordinary people obeyed the ruler-priests, and they, in turn, obeyed the gods. Maya society was organized along the following lines:

Maya Society

Ruler	All public life was controlled by the ruler. There are many stelae and monuments that show rulers in religious, political, and military roles.
Aristocrats	The highest-ranking members of noble families who possessed special knowledge. They controlled trade and commerce and filled the top administrative positions, including the priesthood and the distribution of food supplies. The **batabs,** high-ranking civic administrators, belonged to this class.
Lesser Aristocrats	Lower-ranking priests, scribes, traders, architects, engineers, lower-ranking military officials, and master craftspeople were part of this group. Here, also, were the lesser civic administrators called **ah cuch cab,** who advised the batabs.
Common People	Farmers, laborers, craftspeople, and domestic workers.
Slaves	People in debt, criminals, and prisoners of war. It is believed that most slaves performed domestic duties, worked in the fields, and were used as victims in sacrifices to the gods.

Relief showing a ruler and his royal wife.

Maya society was usually peaceful, even if it was controlled in part by fear. People were afraid to disobey a priest's orders or to refuse to perform a religious ritual, because if they did, the gods would be angry and punish them by causing violent storms, disease, drought, or crop failure.

Over time, Maya society changed: the Formative period evolved into the Classic, then changed to the Postclassic. Even greater change came with the Spanish conquest. As one Maya writer wrote:

"Before the coming of the mighty men and Spaniards there was no robbery with violence, there was no greed and striking down of one's fellow man in his blood, at the cost of the poor man, at the expense of the food and each and everyone...It was the beginning of tribute, the beginning of church dues, the beginning of strife with purse-snatching, the beginning of strife with guns..."

Terra-cotta figurines show a seated man and a standing woman. They were aristocrats who were the highest-ranking members of noble families.

Writing It Down: Recording Things

Writing

The Mayas were the only native American people to develop a full writing system. Their characters were written on pottery, wood, stone, stelae, altars, walls, and on ornaments. The characters are called hieroglyphs, or **glyphs.** Some glyphs were made up of several elements—a main sign and additions to the sign. With these signs, the Mayas could express any idea they wished.

Most Maya inscriptions have now been deciphered by dedicated scholars working over many years. The writing mainly records the passage of time, the actions of prominent individuals, and complex rituals required by the gods.

Books

Maya hieroglyphic writing was also written in books whose pages were a few inches (centimeters) high and several yards (meters) long, and folded like a screen. Each book, or codex, contained recorded knowledge of the Maya. Only three have survived, and they are from the Postclassic period: the Dresden Codex, the Madrid Codex, and the Paris Codex. They are named after the cities in which they are now kept. Most of these books were destroyed by the Christian Spanish, who realized that the writing formed part of Maya religious beliefs and daily life. The Spanish called these books "superstition and lies of the devil" and burned them. In so doing, they destroyed the valuable knowledge of an advanced culture.

Figurine of a woman with a book, or codex.

Recording of Time

To the Mayas, time was sacred and periods of time, which included days, were divine and had to be worshiped. Time was also measured. The Mayas believed that time moved in a huge circle, so that what had happened before would happen again.

Calendar

The Maya calendar and calculation of time was complicated. The Maya calendar was made up of several interlocking cycles of time. The two most important cycles were the vague year and the ceremonial year. The vague year was a solar calendar of 365 days, divided into eighteen months of twenty days each. The eighteen months were followed by five days (considered to be unlucky) belonging to no month.

The ceremonial year (sometimes called Tzolkin) consisted of 260 days. Every day had its omens and associations. These two cycles together were known as "the Calendar Round." One cycle of "the Calendar Round" took fifty-two vague years to complete.

Several types of dates have been found on classic Maya monuments and some monuments carry many dates.

Calculation

The Mayas had a reasonably well-developed mathematical system, which included the idea of zero, long before Europeans did; but they had no decimal system and could not calculate fractions. Their astronomical calculations enabled them to predict eclipses, phases of the moon, and the position of the planet Venus. The priests' knowledge of astronomy was very different from the ideas about the stars and planets that were in the myths and legends.

Stone relief from Yaxchilan bears hieroglyphs made up of gods, animals, and numbers.

Maya Legends

What we know of Maya legends, myths, and literature comes from looking at the Maya religious and ceremonial art, from codices, and from old stories and beliefs that were written down after the Spanish conquest.

The Maize Myth

The thunder god released maize from a mountain to benefit the people. In the blast, some of the maize was scorched, having white, yellow, red, and black ears. These colors are the same as the four world directions.

Maya codices also help us to know about Maya beliefs and gods.

The Creation

The Mayas had a complicated creation myth that tells of man being created and destroyed by his maker. The creator was not happy with man and kept trying to make him perfect.

The Time Legends

The time legends tell of the creation of the uinal, or the twenty-day month. It stands for the divisions of time and the march through eternity. To the Mayas, the time periods and numbers were gods who carried the burden of time upon their backs. Each evening the procession rested, and each morning the time carriers were replaced. There is also a sculpture

that depicts this march showing the bearers lowering their burden.

Legend of the Frogs

This is a story about a young boy who was sent to serve in the house of the Chacs (rain gods). In their house, the Chacs had frogs (called "uo") who were the servants and musicians. When the young boy was asked to sweep the house, he swept out the frogs and then tried to steal one of the Chac's water gourds. In doing so, he spilled some of the water and almost flooded the world.

The *Books of Chilam Balam*

One of the richest sources of knowledge about Maya culture and folklore, which includes some poems and songs, are the *Books of Chilam Balam*. These were about the old traditions and were written down by Maya prophets of the seventeenth and eighteenth centuries. Of the many documents that made up these books, only a few survive today.

Temple of the Magician.

Art and Architecture

The Maya civilization was characterized by monumental art and architecture. There are countless sites. Some have pyramid-temples more than 200 feet (60 meters) high.

Maya lintel (horizontal stone placed over a door) from Yaxchilan that shows a ruler and his wife with symbols of his office.

Beginning in the Formative period, the Mayas built and dated many stone monuments and buildings. Temples, ornaments on architecture, altars, and stelae were constructed as monuments to leaders and gods. Temples were the tallest structures. They usually sat on top of lofty stone pyramids that had flat tops. Many cities had one or more ball courts where a game, played for religious purposes, took place. Scholars believe this game represented the movements of the sun, moon, and other heavenly bodies. The game probably served as entertainment as well.

Palaces, Temples, and Pyramids

Maya palaces differed from the temples and pyramids in that they were lower and had a great many rooms. The royal family probably lived in the palaces along with many elite relatives. Some rooms probably served as administrative offices.

Temples and palaces were often arranged around courts, with stelae and altars built before them. Great stone causeways lead from central plazas in many Maya centers.

Below: the Temple of the Magician at Uxmal.

Opposite: the palace area at Palenque.

At Tikal is a large Maya ceremonial group of buildings, known as the Acropolis, which has white stucco platforms, stairways, and **polychrome** masks. Maya architects often built new buildings on top of older structures.

Copán was the southernmost large cultural center of the Mayas. Copán architecture has many figures of kings, gods, carved stelae, and monuments, as well as a well-preserved ball court. At Copán, a royal dynasty of sixteen kings ruled for about four hundred years.

Palenque lies above the flood plain of the Usumacinta River and has many beautiful temple-pyramids.

Uxmal is a Yucatan city where fine examples of platforms, plazas, pyramid-temples, and palaces are to be found. The site is famed for the delicate stone ornamentation on many of its buildings.

At Bonampak, fine examples of Maya murals show royal ceremonies. Pigments that have been identified include red and pink (red iron oxide); yellow (hydrous iron oxide); black (carbon); blue (origin unknown); and green (by mixing yellow and blue).

Jade belt ornament dated from A.D. 600-800.

Pottery Vessels

Many pottery vessels that have been found are painted with scenes of mythology and royal life and show skill and a variety of detail. Pottery figurines ranging from simple ones of early times to sophisticated lifelike ones of later years show Maya artistic achievement.

Eras of Maya Pottery	
Formative period	Well-made **monochrome** with occasionally two-color polychrome.
Classic period	Polychrome pottery in the Petén.
Postclassic period	Lifelike scenes and geometric designs, also carved pottery made in two-piece molds.

Other types of pottery, which were obtained by trade, have also been found in Maya lands.

The pottery described above was made for the elite and for ceremonies. Most pottery had more practical uses, such as cooking and water storage, and was not elaborately decorated.

Jade Carving

Jade was the stone most highly prized by the Mayas. Exquisite relief designs on jade ornaments show the high level of skill achieved by the Maya artists.

Art styles generally changed through each period of Maya history, but artists in every era worked for the rulers and nobles, creating jewelry and other treasures in jade.

Going Places: Transportation, Exploration, and Communication

Nobility

The nobility ruled Maya society. Only people from this class could be in the government or become priests. The nobility was also in charge of all trade. It was mainly through the nobles that the various Maya centers dealt with each other and kept in touch.

There were many coastal towns, and the island of Cozumel was a major commercial center. Cotton cloth, salt, honey, wax, and slaves were shipped south as far as the Gulf of Honduras in exchange for cacao, precious metals, and feathers.

Vessel with decoration showing Maya dignitary wearing headdress. Goods exchanged in trade often included precious metals and feathers for headdresses worn by dignitaries.

Peasants

The peasants stayed in family groups in one general geographical area. Sometimes the peasants may have traveled long distances to visit shrines and sacred places, such as Chichén Itzá, where they would throw offerings into the cenote of the rain god.

The Maya, as with other ancient American peoples, did not know of the wheel for practical purposes. They did not use it for transportation or to help them with their farming. **Litters** are shown in some art, but these were used by the nobility, who were probably carried when they traveled.

Communication

Archaeologists, by studying the pottery and other artifacts of a civilization, can tell whether the people in different societies communicated and influenced each other. If the pottery from different areas is very similar, it can mean that the people from these areas learned from each other. Pottery from one area that is exactly like pottery from another area indicates that it was traded. Some ancient pottery found in the Maya area in Guatemala and in Yucatan came from central Mexico, hundreds of miles away.

Litters were used to transport nobles.

34

Music, Dancing, and Recreation

Most ancient civilizations included music and dancing as part of their religious ceremonies, as well as for entertainment. We do not know a great deal about Maya songs, music, and dancing. Some of the Maya songs have survived, recorded in the *Books of Chilam Balam*.

The sun god, an important Maya god, was also the patron of music and poetry. Musical instruments shown in Maya art include drums, long horns, and rattles. Pottery objects that have been found include whistles and flutes.

Dances

The old music and dances used in Maya religious ceremonies were forbidden by the Christian Spanish and were replaced with Spanish religious music.

The murals at Bonampak show several ceremonial dances in which masked dancers are dressed to look like gods. Other dances were thought to have been used to ensure the success of crops and hunting. Before the dance, performers had to observe certain rituals, which included periods of **fasting**. When the ceremony included sacrifice, the victim, and his or her relatives and friends, were believed to be participants in the dance. In spite of Spanish attempts to stop this practice, some of these sacrificial dances lived on for a century, after the Spanish conquest, as part of the culture of the Quiché and Zutuhil peoples.

The Ball Game

There are ball courts at Tikal, Copán, Chichén Itzá, and other sites. The ball game was played with a solid rubber ball, perhaps at times for recreation, but mainly as a religious ceremony. No one knows exactly what the rules were or

Cylindrical vessel showing figure wearing the costume of a ball player.

how many players were on each team. Losers may have been sacrificed. Some ball courts have rings along the walls resembling goal rings; others have markers along the center of the floor or along the sides. Some ball courts are perfectly plain. Some courts have temples nearby where players may have made offerings to the gods before and after a game.

Wars and Battles

The Mayas were generally peaceful, but at times they engaged in warfare. These wars were usually fought between neighboring city-states. Classic-period murals at Bonampak illustrate two groups of Maya warriors fighting. A later scene shows captives brought before the ruler of Bonampak. They were probably sacrificed in an important ceremony. However,

Chichén Itzá—the Temple of the Warriors.

there were probably more raids than battles, and more battles than long, full-scale wars.

Maya settlements, for the most part, remained peaceful, enjoying such relationships as trade and political alliances. However, archaeologists have discovered that at some sites, protective walls and defensive moats surround a city. These show that the Mayas sometimes felt the need to defend themselves from enemy attack. During late Classic and Postclassic times, more emphasis was placed on defense and military matters. Murals at Chichén Itzá show a battle, and sculpture shows warriors wearing various kinds of military headdresses. In Yucatan, Mayapán became the capital of a vast allied area. Rulers of the city-states that lay within the alliance were required to live almost as captives within the crowded walled city so that their territories could be easily controlled.

Though the Mayas had soldiers, little is known about them. They may have been farmers who served as part-time soldiers, taking part in raids or battles only when the ruler required their service.

Weapons

Maya weapons included bows and arrows, and spears and spearthrowers. Pieces of obsidian, or volcanic glass, were set into wooden war clubs. The Mayas also were able to make very thin blades, daggers, and spear points from flint. (Flint was available to the Mayas of the lowlands, while obsidian was only found in the highlands.)

A peculiar weapon used by the highland Mayas was a hornet bomb. Hornets' nests were kept and hurled at the enemy. How these nests were kept, stored, and transported is not known.

Terra-cotta figurine of a warrior.

Astronomical Calculations and the Calendar

The Maya calendar, based on astronomical observations, was a great intellectual achievement. With the calendar came the ability to understand and measure time, and even to predict certain events, such as solar eclipses and the orbital cycle of the planet Venus. These calculations using astronomy and basic arith-

Pyramid of the Magician at Uxmal—in the building of pyramids, the Mayas understood the problems of stress and strain, and the pull of gravity.

Opposite: Maya architecture was often advanced and sophisticated. Stone façades, such as this one, often were covered with decoration.

metic were remarkably accurate. For example, the Mayas, in calculating the cycle of Venus, showed an error of only one day in slightly over 6,000 years of calculation. This is especially remarkable when we consider that the Mayas had very little information about the nature of the universe and no sophisticated observation instruments.

39

Writing

Today, scholars are able to decipher most of the surviving inscriptions. In doing so, they recognize that Maya writing was far more advanced than the writing of any neighboring culture. The Maya writing system was a complete system, combining picture symbols with phonetic signs. This allowed the Mayas to develop a language rich in synonyms and homonyms.

Unique Buildings

Maya architecture was often more advanced than the architecture of neighboring peoples. It demanded great engineering skill to build the structures the Mayas built. It also required the ability to manufacture and use concrete expertly and to understand the problems of stress and strain, and the pull of gravity.

Stelae

The Mayas are noted for these kinds of monuments. Many cities are known to have erected these monuments, which bear inscriptions that relate to Maya history.

Use of Rubber

The Mayas made use of rubber for balls long before any civilization in Europe did. However, knowledge of rubber and its uses was common to most ancient peoples of Central America and Mexico. They probably learned of its use from earlier cultures.

Maya Blue

This was a bright color used by the Mayas in such art as murals and pottery, especially during the Classic period. Recent discoveries show that other peoples also used it.

Jade Carving

Maya craftspeople, through patience and a highly developed skill, made some of the most intricate and beautiful jade pieces. Jade was a symbol of wealth. A jade bead was often placed in the mouth of a dead person of rank. It also had religious meaning and was sometimes used in sacrifice and divination.

Roads

The Mayas had no wheeled vehicles, yet they built roads. These roads were built solely for great religious processions or for pilgrimages to shrines.

Farming Skills

The Mayas possessed exceptional farming skills. They planted according to the arrival of the rainy season. In addition, in some areas they built raised fields and were skilled at draining land and building irrigation canals.

Why the Civilization Declined

Beginning in about A.D. 790, the advanced lowland Maya civilization went into a decline from which it never recovered. After A.D. 918, no more stelae were erected in lowland Mexico. By the tenth century, the civic core of every southern Maya city was abandoned. Most Mayas moved to farms and villages. Some attempts were made to repair broken stelae in Postclassic times when some of the centers were occupied again. The northern cities were the last to decline.

No satisfactory explanations of the decline have been given, but there are several theories. One theory suggests that the people left the centers in fear of earthquakes, hurricanes, or disease, but no clear evidence proves this. Others suggest that crop failures due to pests and disease may have been the cause or that overfarming rendered the land useless, but both theories seem doubtful. Another explanation suggests that invasions drove the people from the land, but evidence suggests otherwise.

Scholars suggest that perhaps the peasants revolted against the aristocracy and nobility, but without the knowledge of leaders and administrators, the peasants failed in an attempt to govern themselves. In any case, the likelihood is that the lines of communication between the large Maya centers were broken. Since communication was essential to survival, the decline could not be stopped.

Perhaps the real reason will turn up when more Maya inscriptions are deciphered. Undiscovered inscriptions still stand in the forests of Mexico and Central America.

The people of Guatemala today, descendants of the ancient Maya.

Glossary

Agouti A shorthaired, rabbitlike rodent.

Ah cuch cab Lesser civic administrators who advised the batab.

Atole A cornmeal gruel that was taken with chili pepper as the first meal of the day.

Balche A drink made from honey and the bark of a native tree that was consumed in large quantities during festivals.

Batab High-ranking civic administrator.

Cacao A tree that produces a chocolate bean, which is used to make a drink.

Ceiba Wild cotton tree that grows in the tropical rain forests, which the Mayas once inhabited. This tree was sacred to the Mayas.

Cenote A natural well formed beneath the porous limestone, which covered much of the area of Yucatan, providing the sole source of water. Some cenotes were considered sacred.

Chili A small red fruit that is very hot to the taste, used by the Mayas in most food.

Curassow Large bird found in South America. It resembles the turkey in appearance and is often domesticated.

Divination An attempt to discover the future or to decide the outcome of events by supernatural means or a prophecy based on chance. Divination did not use logical reasoning.

Excavation A place where materials such as earth and debris have been removed carefully to uncover ruins or remains from earlier times.

Fasting Going without food, not eating.

Genealogy The study of families through their ancestry or family trees.

Glyph A pictograph or form of hieroglyph used by the Mayas and carved on their monuments and buildings.

Hmen Men who were both sorcerers and medicine men; both prophets and healers of disease.

Iron pyrite A lustrous, pale, brass-yellow mineral, sometimes called fools' gold. It was used by the highland Mayas for mirrors.

Jade A hard, green gemstone used as an ornamental stone for jewelry and carvings.

Limestone A rock consisting mainly of calcium carbonate, which is very porous.

Litter A vehicle carried by men. It consisted of a seat or couch for the passenger suspended between two shafts. Maya carvings show nobles being transported in this way by slaves. Litters have been found buried in tombs.

Maguey A South American cactus with spiny leaves from which a fiber was obtained and used to make coarse twine that could be woven.

Monochrome Decorated in one color.

Mural A decoration painted or carved on a wall.

Obsidian A volcanic glass, usually dark in color, used by the Mayas to fashion sharp knives and spear points.

Ossuary A burial place.

Peccary A large nocturnal animal resembling a pig.

Polychrome Decorated in many colors.

Posol A mixture of water and sour dough carried in gourds to the fields for food during the day.

Sacrifice An offering (animal, plant, human, or material possession) made to the god(s). The Mayas practiced human sacrifice.

Sisal Fiber prepared from the leaves of the agave plant and used for cordage, ropes, and clothing.

Sloth A slow-moving, tree-dwelling mammal that lives in the rain forests.

Specular hematite An iron oxide mineral found in red earthly masses and used by the Mayas to create red paint, a color frequently in use.

Stele An upright slab or pillar of stone bearing an inscription, sculptural design, and usually a date. Plural *stelae*.

Tamale A food made of crushed maize and minced meat, seasoned with peppers, wrapped in maize husks, and steamed.

Tortilla A thin, round, flat cake made from maize or corn meal and baked on a flat stone or earthenware surface. It was eaten with beans, meat, and chilies.

Trogon Bird found in tropical and subtropical regions notable for its brilliant plumage; this bird belongs to the same family as the quetzal.

Volcanic tuff A rock of volcanic origin of compacted or cemented volcanic ash and dust. It was used to make first-rate temper for Maya potters because it could bear relatively high firing temperatures.

The Mayas: Some Famous People and Places

TIKAL

Tikal, in northern Petén, was the mightiest of all Maya centers. It had about 3,000 structures ranging from tiny mounds to great temple-pyramids, all within an area of 6 square miles (16 square kilometers). It was the largest Maya city and ceremonial center in the southern lowlands. Stelae found here date from the third to ninth centuries A.D., but only a few of these have been deciphered. At least ten thousand people are thought to have lived in Tikal at its height of achievement in A.D. 700; but the surrounding area, with a population of 50,000, also regarded Tikal as its center.

COPÁN

Copán was a Maya city and an important center for Maya art and astronomy. It had many stelae with portrait sculptures and many of its buildings had friezes. Copán flourished during the Classic period. It was in Copán that astronomers calculated the most accurate solar calendar produced by the Mayas. The ruins of Copán were discovered by Spanish explorers in the early sixteenth century.

The ruined city was restored between 1936 and 1950.

UAXACTUN

This Maya city in the southern lowlands was not nearly as large as Tikal. Many ceremonial buildings were constructed here, including a great temple with giant stucco masks. Many major buildings date from the Formative period. The city was abandoned in the tenth century.

CHICHÉN ITZÁ

This is a ruined Maya city built in the sixth century around two large cenotes (deep wells). The name is derived from chi (Maya for "mouths"), chen (Maya for "wells"), and Itzá, the name of the tribe that settled here. Hence the name means "mouths of the wells of the Itzá." Earliest structures dating from the Classic period include the Akabtzib (House of the Dark Writing), the Chichanchob (Red House), the House of the Deer, the Iglesia (Church), and the Monjas (Nunnery). The city was invaded in the tenth century by the people who constructed the great pyramid, Castillo, the ball court, the High Priest's Grave, the Colonnade, and the Temple of the Warriors, all thought to have been completed in the early Postclassic period from A.D. 900 to 1200.

At Chichén Itzá, gold and jade ornaments, as well as humans, were sacrificed by being thrown into one of the city's cenotes.

BISHOP LANDA

Diego de Landa was bishop of Yucatan. He arrived from Spain to serve in the Monastery of Izamal in 1549. He wrote *Relación de las Cosas de Yucatán* (*On the Things of Yucatan*) in about 1566. This work is the best description of the Postclassic religion in Yucatan and contains a great deal of other information about later Maya life.

He was, however, determined to stamp out all aspects of the native religion and had any pagan worshipers severely beaten. He also had many books destroyed at the Mani library that were written by native priests prior to the conquest. He maintained that the books "contained nothing in which there was not to be seen superstition and lies of the devil, we burned them all."

HERNANDEZ DE CORDOBA

Hernandez de Cordoba was a Spanish leader whose ships reached Yucatan in the early spring of 1517. A fleet of ten native long boats, each containing up to forty natives, went to meet the Spanish and some boarded Cordoba's ship. The next day a party escorted Cordoba and his party ashore into an ambush. The Spanish, armed with muskets, managed to flee to one of the temples. There they plundered much gold and many other valuable objects, which they took to their waiting ships, and sailed from the place that was later to be called Cape Catoche.

Cordoba's ships proceeded along the Yucatan Peninsula, where they encountered more people who regarded them as enemies and attacked them. Cordoba eventually set sail for Cuba to begin to tell the world about the Maya people, their cities, and their wealth.

JUAN DE GRIJALVA

Encouraged by Cordoba's reports, Governor Diego Velasquez sent out a second expedition to Yucatan in 1518, under the command of Juan de Grijalva. This expedition made landfall at Cozumel on Yucatan's east coast. From here they followed Cordoba's previous route. At Champoton, his party was also attacked by the Mayas. Those of this expedition also saw the wealthy Maya cities but found them deserted.

PALENQUE

This is a modern name for one of the ruined Maya cities. The original name is not known. The Mayas here had used a plaster to finish the walls of their buildings. The Temple of Inscriptions, with its many hieroglyphics, is one of the largest structures in the city. In 1952 a crypt was discovered under the temple and in it were the remains of a person covered in jade ornaments. The person buried here may have been a priest-ruler of the seventh century.

UXMAL

Uxmal is a ruined Maya city in Yucatan. This city continued to be occupied after the lowland Maya cities declined. This city was also abandoned about 1450. The ruins cover about 160 acres (60 hectares), and the main buildings are the Temple of the Magician, the Nunnery Quadrangle, the Governor's Palace, the House of Turtles, and the House of Pigeons.

LAKE PETÉN ITZA

Lake Petén Itza is a depression about 164 feet (50 meters) deep and about 15 miles (24 kilometers) wide (east to west). This was once the stronghold of the Itza Maya, who were not conquered by the Spanish until 1697.

Index